SCINTILLATING SCARECROWS

KATHERINE E. TAPLEY-MILTON

Published by

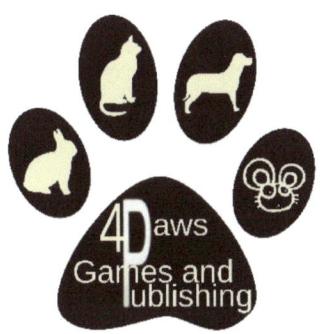

Humboldt, Saskatchewan, Canada

Scintillating Scarecrows

Written and Created by Katherine E. Tapley-Milton

Photos by Katherine E. Tapley-Milton

Cover Art by 4 Paws Games and Publishing

Edited by Kathrine E. Tapley-Milton and 4 Paws Games and Publishing

Formatted and Published by 4 Paws Games and Publishing
Published October 2017 First Edition
ISBN 13: 978-1-988345-53-6

ISBN 10: 1988345537

Copyright © 2017 by Katherine E. Tapley-Milton
All Rights Reserved
Published by 4 Paws Games and Publishing
P.O. Box 444
Humboldt, Saskatchewan, Canada S0K 2A0
http://www.4-Paws-Games-and-Publishing.ca
Publishing logo and name copyright © 2016
All Rights Reserved

The publisher is not responsible for the book, website, or social media (or its content) that is not owned by the publisher. All legal matters are to be taken up by the author as the publisher holds no responsibilities.

The author and publisher have made every effort

to ensure the accuracy of the information within this book was correct at time of publication. The author and publisher acknowledge that not every location is in the book at this time.

No part of this publication may be reproduced, distributed, or transmitted in any form or by any means, including photocopying, recording, or other electronic or mechanical methods, without the prior written permission of the publisher, except in the case of brief quotations embodied in critical reviews and certain other non-commercial uses permitted by copyright law.

Attention: Permission C/O
Katherine E. Tapley-Milton
18 Squire Street
Sackville, New Brunswick E4L 4K9

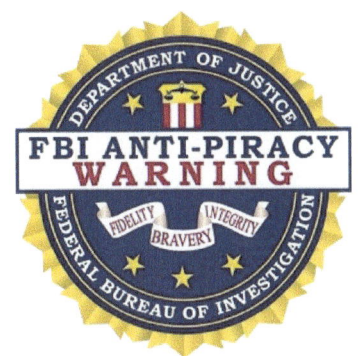

Other Books by Katherine E. Tapley-Milton

Big Stuff in the Maritimes Series

1-3

Other Books

Kathy's Down East Christmas Cookbook

Mother Tapley's Recipe Book: Tasty Down East Cooking

The Disappearing Mailboxes of New Brunswick and Nova Scotia: A Touring of Mailboxes

Old Boats and Old Quotes

The Adventures of the Three Mouse-Breath-Kateers

The Adventures of Sir Lancelot the Cat

Scintillating Scarecrows

And more.

Find Katherine Online

Website
http://authorkatherinetapleymilton.weebly.com
Facebook
https://www.facebook.com/KatherineETapleyMilton
Amazon Authors Central Page
https://www.amazon.com/Katherine-Tapley-Milton/e/B00CP8EBR8

Like the book? Please post a review online where you bought it!

INTRODUCTION TO SCINTILLATING SCARECROWS

What is a scarecrow? Thom Sokoloski and Jenny McCowen comment, "The scarecrow is a disposable figure/effigy made of cast-offs, as well as sacred materials, imbued through ceremony and set up on cultivated land or within an architecture to prevent the incursion of wild or unknown nature, be it real or mythical. Scarecrows are inhabitants of the periphery.

They can conjure a mystery that can be experienced outside of time by stirring the imagination with unknowns.... Farming has always been subject to the whims of nature, and the farmer has always lived at the mercy of a capricious environment. A sudden drought or flood could result in starvation. An infestation of pests, birds and carnivores could devastate crops and livestock; a plague could destroy everything, and more importantly, life.

Scarecrows served as effigies to prevent or raise fear in the perception of an invader, to subvert or halt infringement. Like the gargoyles on the Gothic cathedral, the scarecrow could be likened to a hex to protect the farm from harm and keep evil spirits away." [1]

Today, it is hard to find a scarecrow in backyard gardens or larger scale farms. People

[1] http://thomasandguinevere.com/overview-scarecrows/

put their faith in mechanical gizmos to guard their crops or modern pesticides to guarantee pest control. However, the scarecrow still has a mystique about it. There have been many horror movies about scarecrows, numerous children's books written, and communities around the world hold scarecrow festivals in the fall. Many of the scarecrows in this book are from the Scarecrow Festival in Mahone Bay, Nova Scotia, Canada.

ACKNOWLEDGEMENTS

Many thanks go to the Mahone Bay Scarecrow Festival and their dedicated volunteers who have made over 200 scarecrows that were free to photograph this summer. This festival has been going for 21 years and draws big crowds of parents, their children, and their dogs. Along with the scarecrows there were yard sales, antique sales, and interesting places to eat. The whole town of Mahone Bay is very picturesque and a delight for tourists. May the scare-crow festival keep going another 21 years.

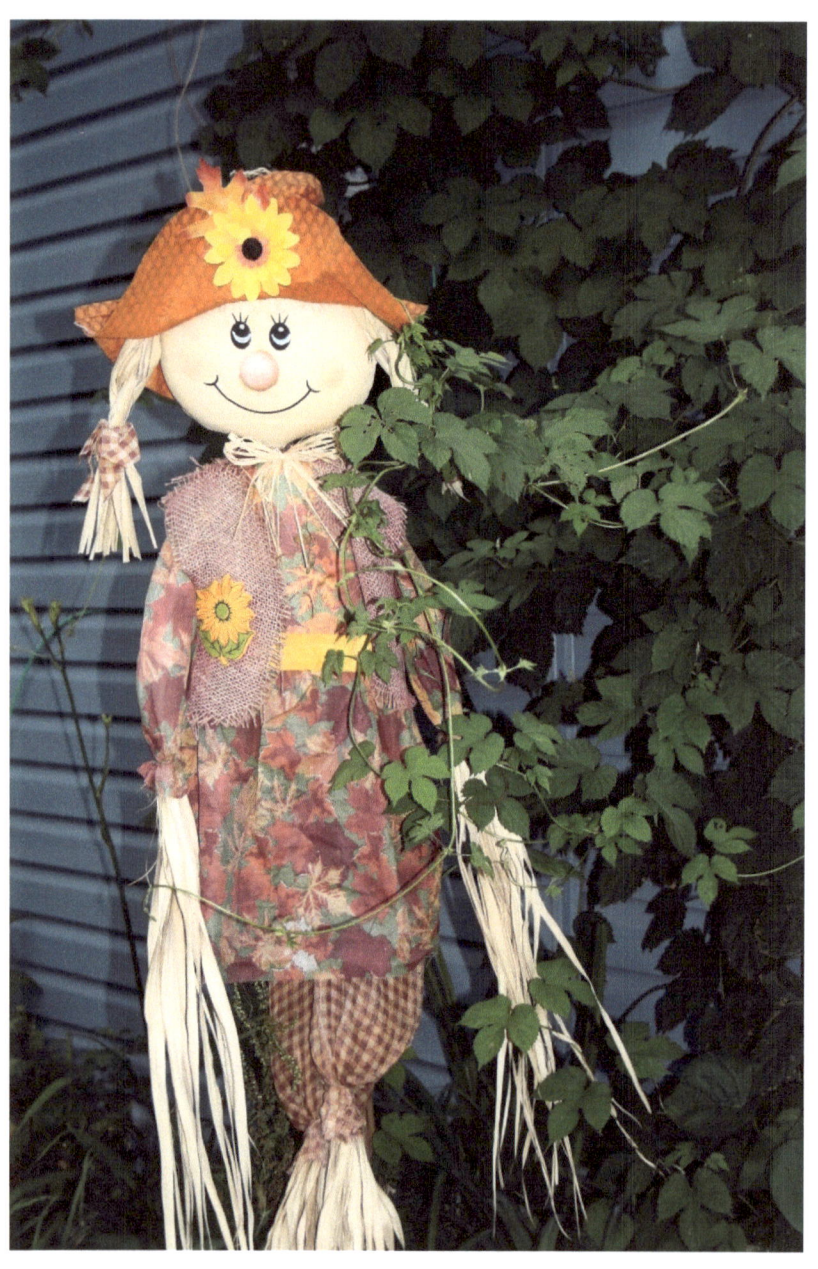

THE EGYPTIANS WERE THE FIRST PEOPLE TO USE SCARECROWS. THEY PUT THEM IN THEIR WHEAT CROPS TO KEEP THE QUAIL OUT AND PUT NETTING OVER WOODEN FRAMES.

http://historybecauseitshere.weebly.com/scarecrows-historically-speaking.html

HOW TO MAKE A KNITTED SCARECROW CAN BE FOUND AT:

https://www.etsy.com/market/knitted_scarecrow

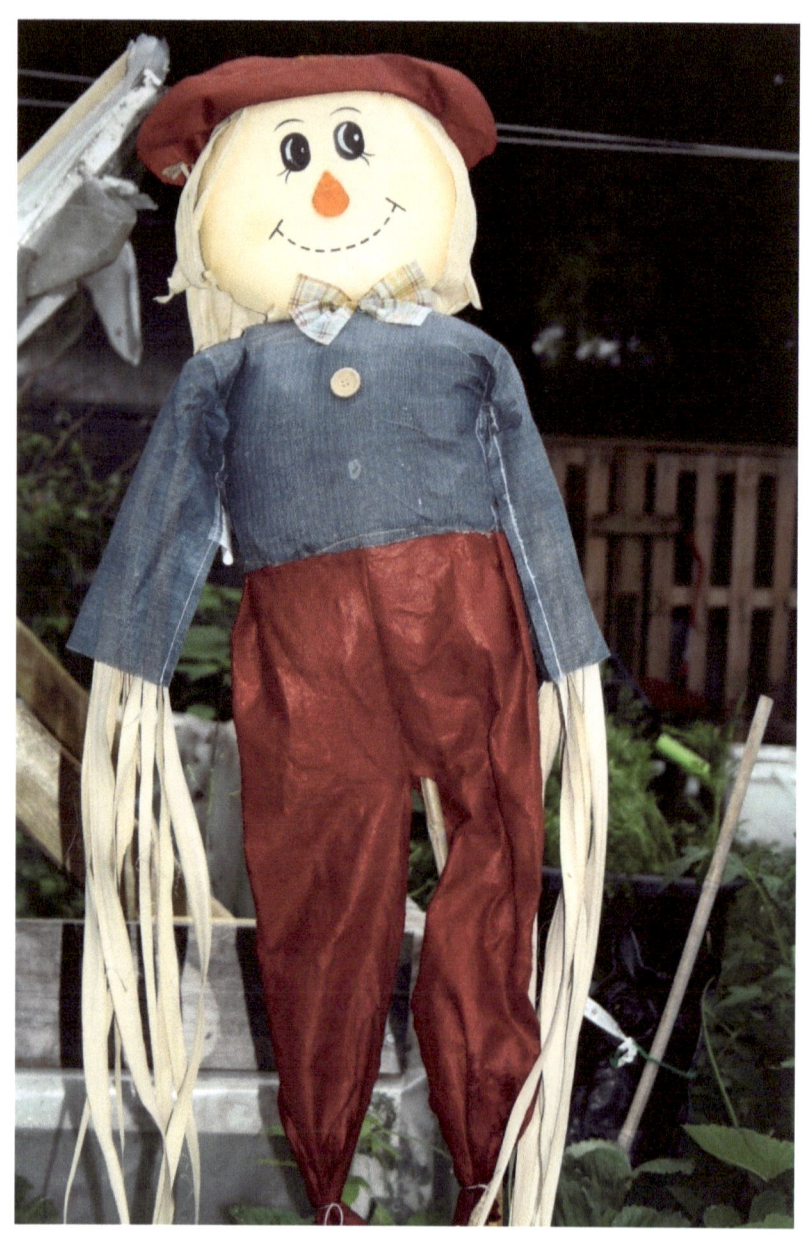

MOST SCARECROWS ARE IN THE SHAPE OF A HUMAN, BUT SOME ARE IN DIFFERENT SHAPES LIKE CROWS, SHEEP, PUMPKINS, ETC.

THE MOST FAMOUS SCARECROW WAS IN "THE WIZARD OF OZ." THE ACTOR WAS RAY BOLGER WHO ALSO PLAYED THE RANCH HAND "HUNK."

"SOHDO KAMI" IS THE NAME FOR THE GOD OF THE SCARECROWS, IN JAPANESE MYTHOLOGY.

"FORMIDOPHOBIA" IS THE NAME FOR THE FEAR OF SCARECROWS.

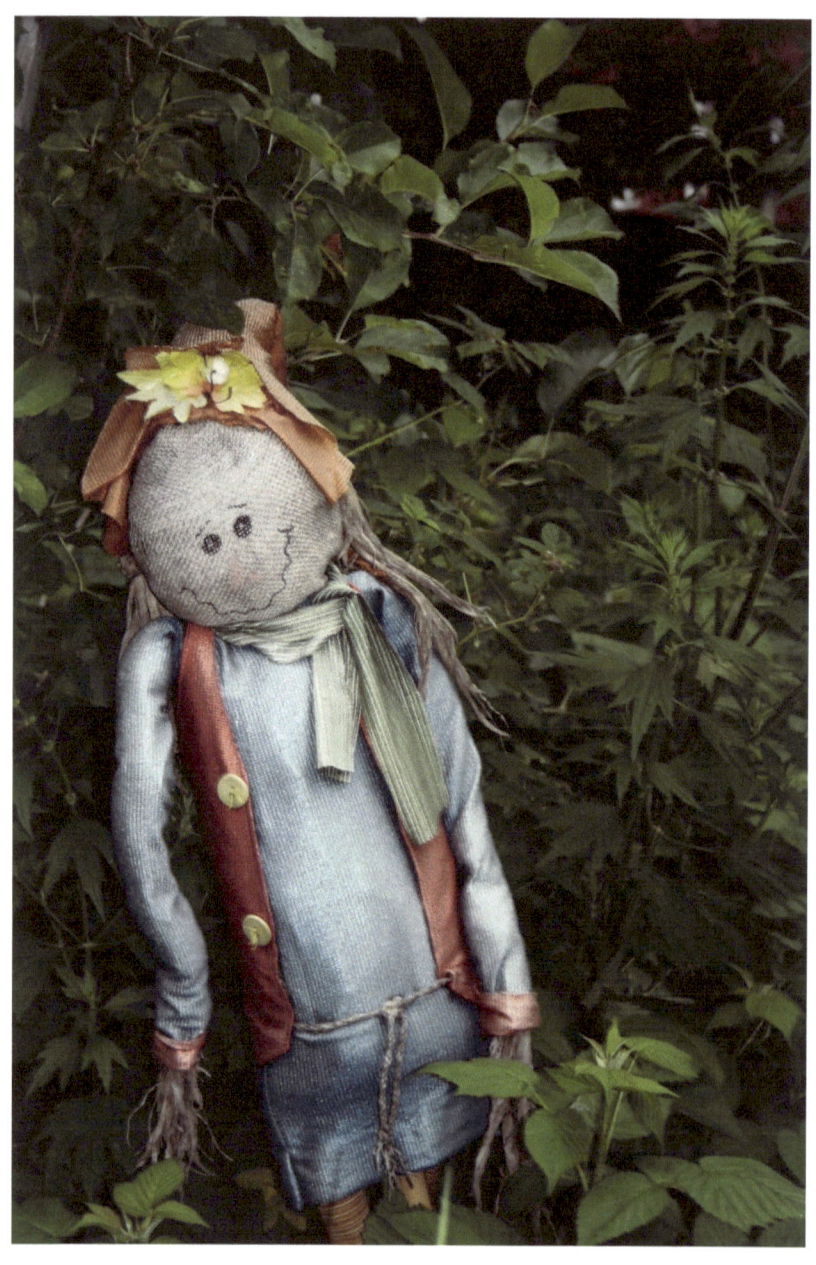

"ITS SYMBOLISM IS UNIVERSAL, BUT THE ORIGINAL SCARECROWS WERE NOTHING LIKE THE NOW FAMILIAR STRAW-STUFFED ICON OF HALLOWEEN. SCARECROWS, SOMETIMES BEARING AN ANIMAL SKULL OR ROTTING PRODUCE, WERE PLACED IN FIELDS IN THE SPRING AND WERE BURNED AFTER THE AUTUMN HARVEST IN CELEBRATION, THEIR ASHES RETURNING NUTRIENTS OF POTASSIUM AND NITROGEN TO THE SOIL."

(https://modernfarmer.com/2014/05/scarecrow-history-effigy/)

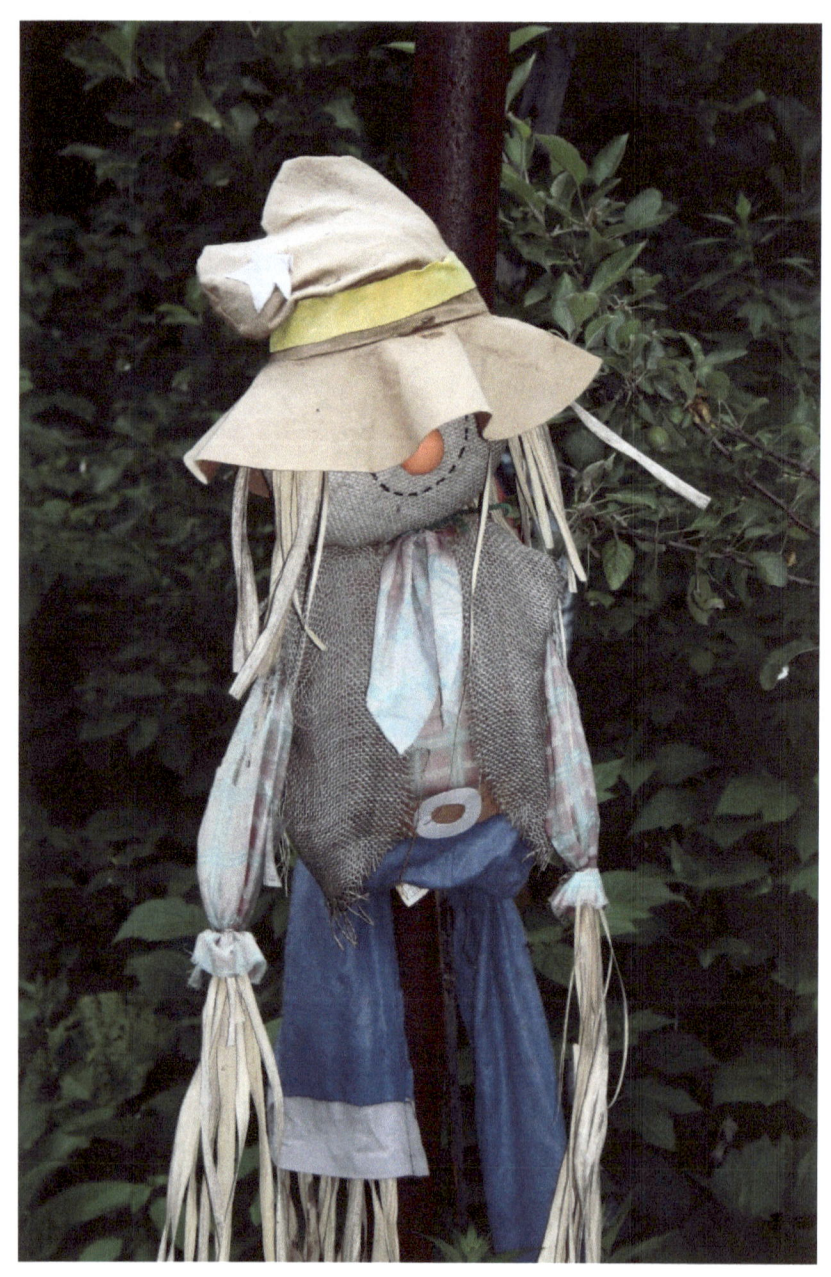

AFTER THE BLACK DEATH AND THE SCARCITY OF CHILDREN IN THE 1600'S, ADULTS WERE SENT OUT INTO THE FIELDS TO SCARE AWAY BIRDS FROM THE CROPS. PERHAPS THIS IS WHY SCARECROWS ALWAYS LOOK LIKE ADULTS. THE HUMAN SCARECROWS STAYED IN A STRAW HUT.

IN BELBROUGHTON, WORCESTERSHIRE, ENGLAND THERE IS AN ANNUAL SCARECROW FESTIVAL THAT IS THE BIGGEST ONE HELD IN BRITAIN. IT IS ALWAYS ON SEPTEMBER 23RD AND 24TH.

ON THE NATIONAL FOREST ADVENTURE FARM IN THE UNITED KINGDOM, ON AUGUST 7TH, 2014 THERE WERE 3,812 SCARECROWS BROUGHT TOGETHER, WHICH SET A RECORD.

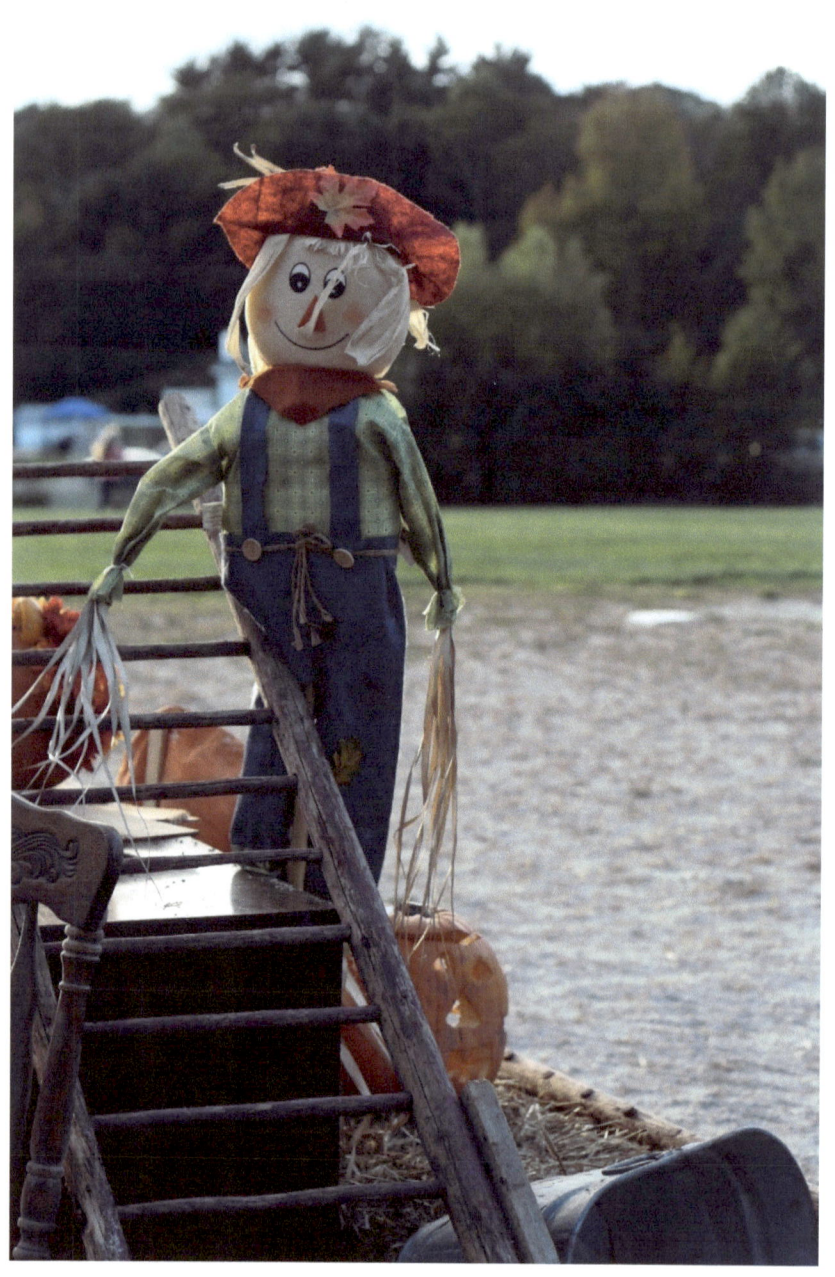

IN JAPANESE MYTHOLOGY THE SCARECROW IS CALLED "KUBIKO" AND HE IS SUPPOSED TO KNOW EVERYTHING, BECAUSE HE STANDS OUTDOORS ALL DAY.

"MODERN SCARECROWS SELDOM TAKE A HUMAN SHAPE. ON CALIFORNIA FARMLAND, HIGHLY REFLECTIVE ALUMINIZED PET FILM RIBBONS ARE TIED TO THE PLANTS TO CREATE SHIMMERS FROM THE SUN. ANOTHER APPROACH ARE AUTOMATIC NOISE GUNS POWERED WITH PROPANE GAS. IN THE SOUTHERN APPALACHIANS ANOTHER COMMON METHOD OF SCARING OFF CROWS WAS USE OF A DEAD CROW HUNG UPSIDE DOWN FROM A POLE."

(Article Source: http://EzineArticles.com/555669)

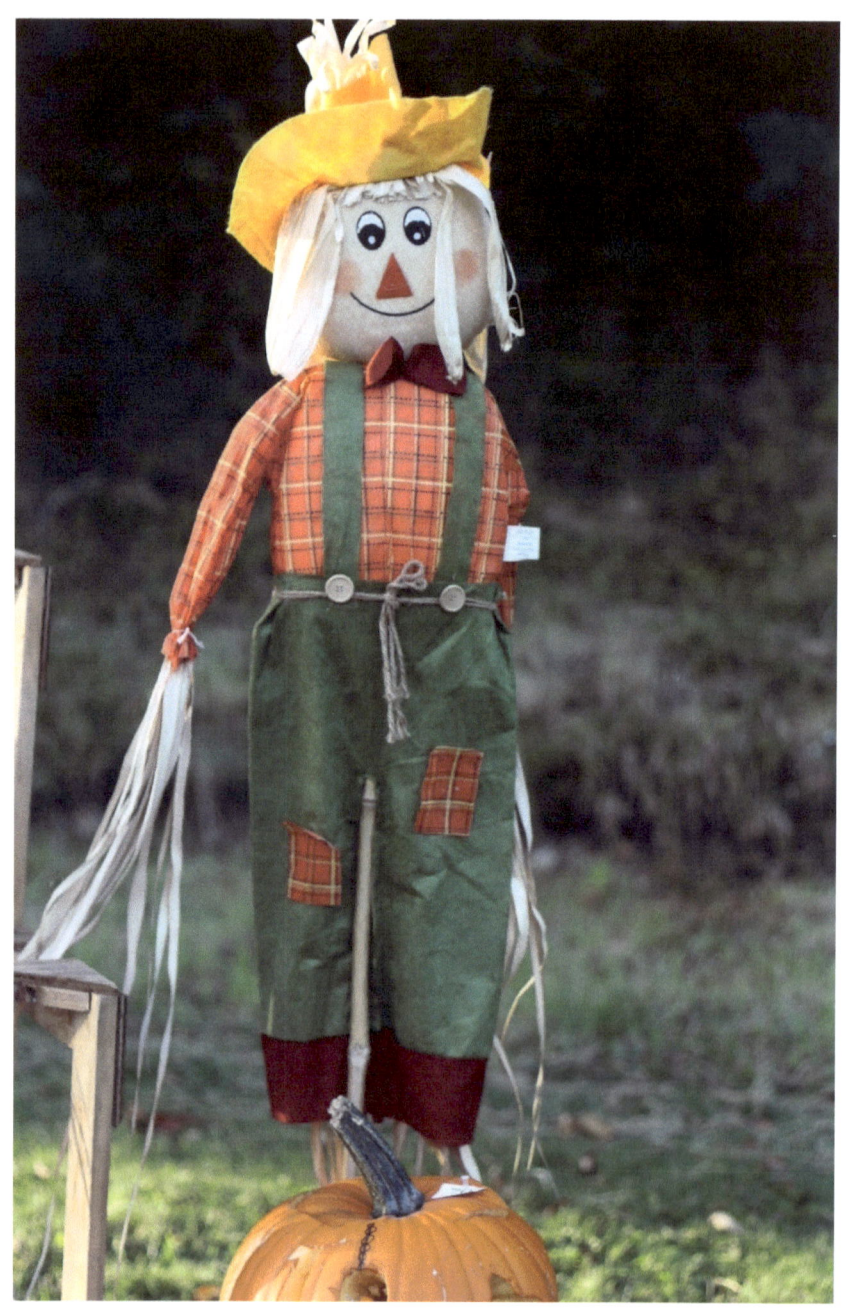

"JACK-A-LENT" REFERS TO A SCARECROW IN ONE OF SHAKESPEARE'S PLAYS CALLED, "THE MERRY WIVES OF WINDSOR" AND HE REFERS TO ONE OF THE STRAW DOLLS THAT HAS THINGS THROWN AT IT ALL DURING LENT.

"JAPANESE FARMERS ... BEGAN MAKING SCARECROWS TO PROTECT THEIR RICE FIELDS. THE FARMERS HUNG OLD RAGS, MEAT, AND FISH BONES FROM BAMBOO POLES IN THEIR FIELDS AND THEN SET THEM ON FIRE. THE SMELL WAS SO BAD THAT BIRDS, AND ALL OTHER LIVING CREATURES, STAYED FAR AWAY FROM THE CROPS."

(http://www.strange-facts.info/interesting-facts-about-scarecrows)

AL PACINO STARRED IN THE ROLE, "SCARECROW" THAT WAS RELEASED IN 1973. IT IS ABOUT AN EX-OFFENDER WHO PARTNERS WITH A HOMELESS EX-SAILER.

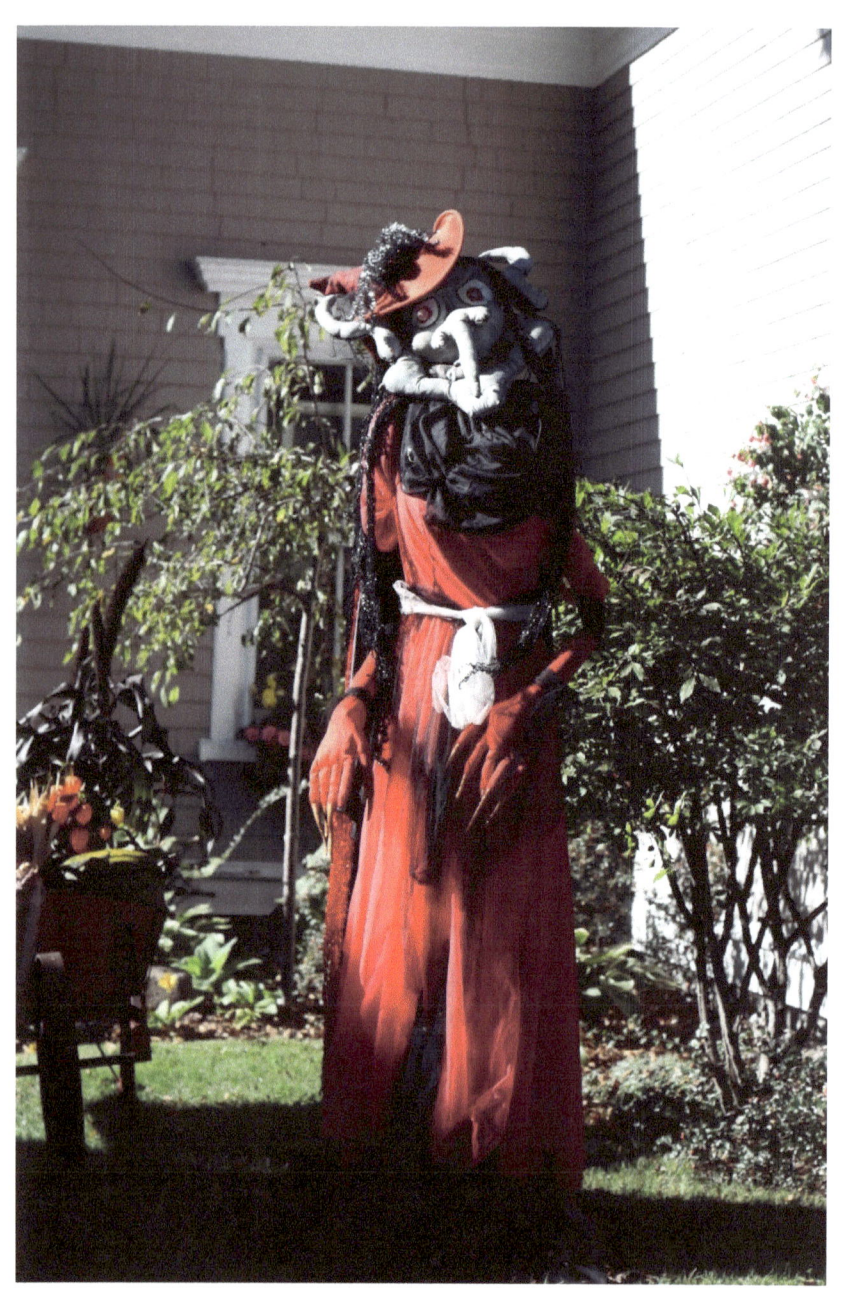

SCARECROW SONG

To be sung to "There's a Tavern in the Town"

There's a scarecrow in the town;

In the town.

Where the birdies sit them down,

Sits them down.

The farmer doesn't want any crows

Eating up his garden rows.

When its time to harvest corn;

Harvest corn

You have to rise in early morn'

Early morn'

And break your back all day in the sun

But at dusk your scarecrow's work is done.

Katherine Tapley-Milton

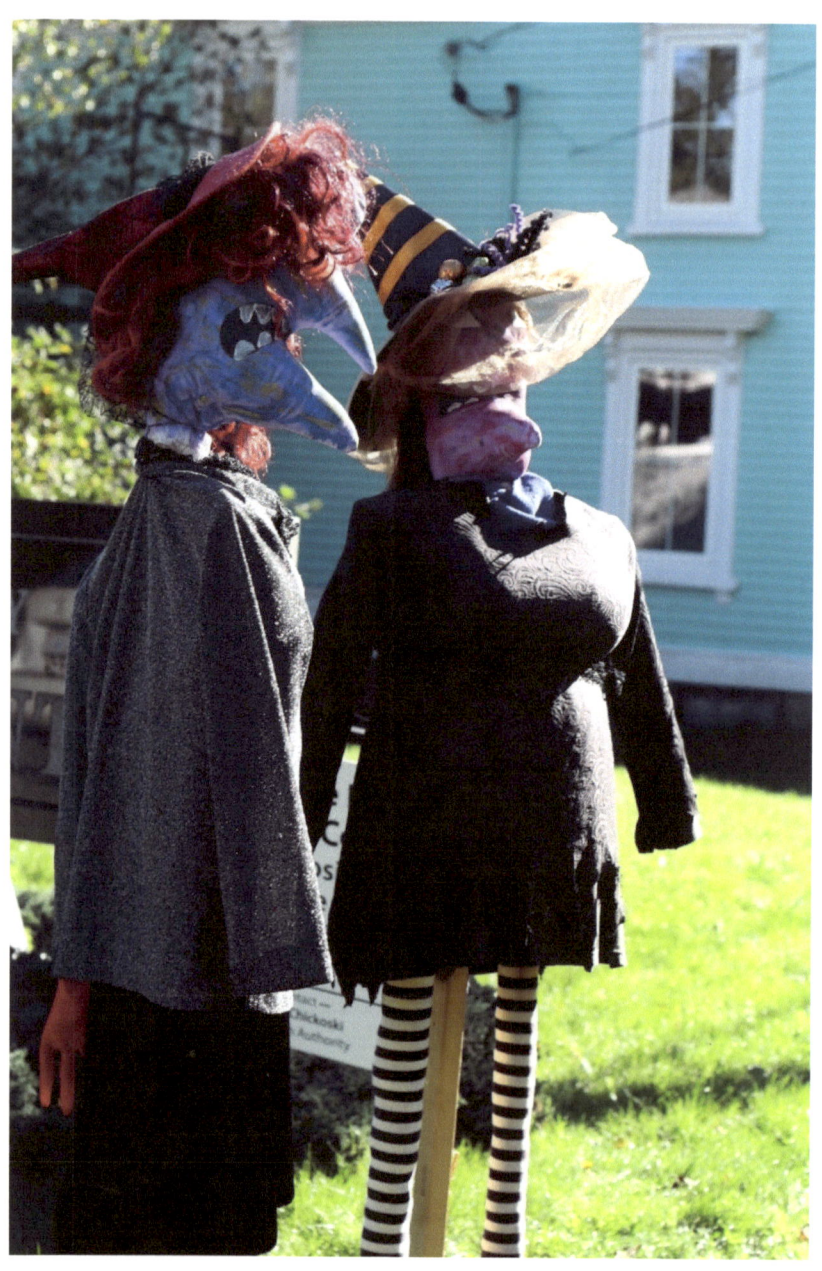

"THE WIZARD OF OZ" BY L. FRANK BAUM, HAS THE MOST FAMOUS SCARECROW OF ALL TIME IN IT. HE HAS STRAW FOR BRAINS, BUT HELPS DOROTHY FIND THE WIZARD.

A SCARECROW IS A DECOY IN YOUR DREAMS. "DO YOU WANT TO DECEIVE? IS THERE A REASON WHY? ADDITIONALLY, THERE MAY BE A PERSON AVAILABLE TRYING TO FOOL YOU. END UP BEING ON YOUR GUARD. THE SCARECROW REPRESENTS THE QUALITIES OF PEOPLE THAT FAIL TO MAKE YOU HAPPY AND YOU USUALLY REJECT THESE PEOPLE. ITS APPEARANCE IN YOUR DREAM IS A DEMAND TO CORRECT YOUR NEGATIVE JUDGMENT."

(https://www.auntyflo.com/dream-dictionary/scarecrow)

THERE IS AN EXTREMELY EVIL SCARECROW IN "BATMAN RETURNS" (2005). THE SCARECROW CONSPIRES WITH THE *LEAGUE OF SHADOWS* TO CORRUPT THE CITY WHICH BATMAN IS SUPPOSED TO SAVE.

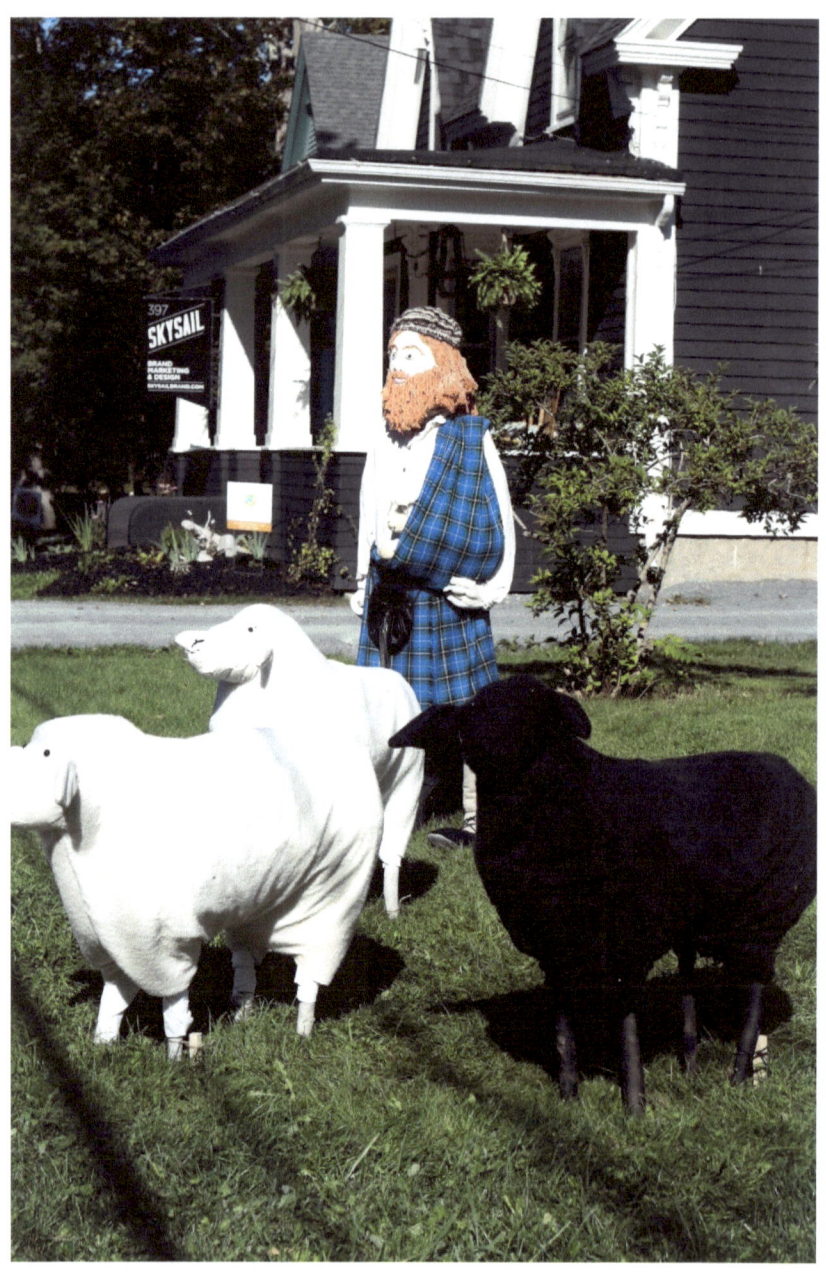

THE GREEKS IN 2,500 BC. UTILIZED SCARECROWS TO PROTECT THEIR CROPS. THEY WERE SUPPOSED TO LOOK LIKE PRIAPUS WHO WAS THE SON OF DIONYSUS AND APHRODITE. THE LATTER WAS SUPPOSED TO BE SO HOMELY THAT SHE WOULD SCARE ANYTHING AWAY. THE GREEK SCARECROWS HAD A CLUB IN ONE OF HER HANDS AND A SCYTHE IN ANOTHER TO SYMBOLIZE HARVEST.

"A SCARECROW IS A TOTEM OF DEATH AND FEAR, BUT IT SIMULTANEOUSLY HOLDS THE OPPOSITE SYMBOLISM OF HOPE AND PROSPERITY. ... SCARECROWS ARE MEANT TO FRIGHTEN AWAY CROWS FROM THE CROPS, WHICH IS WHY THEY ARE OFTEN EERIE AND FRIGHTENING ..."

(http://dreamstop.com/scarecrow-dream-symbol/)

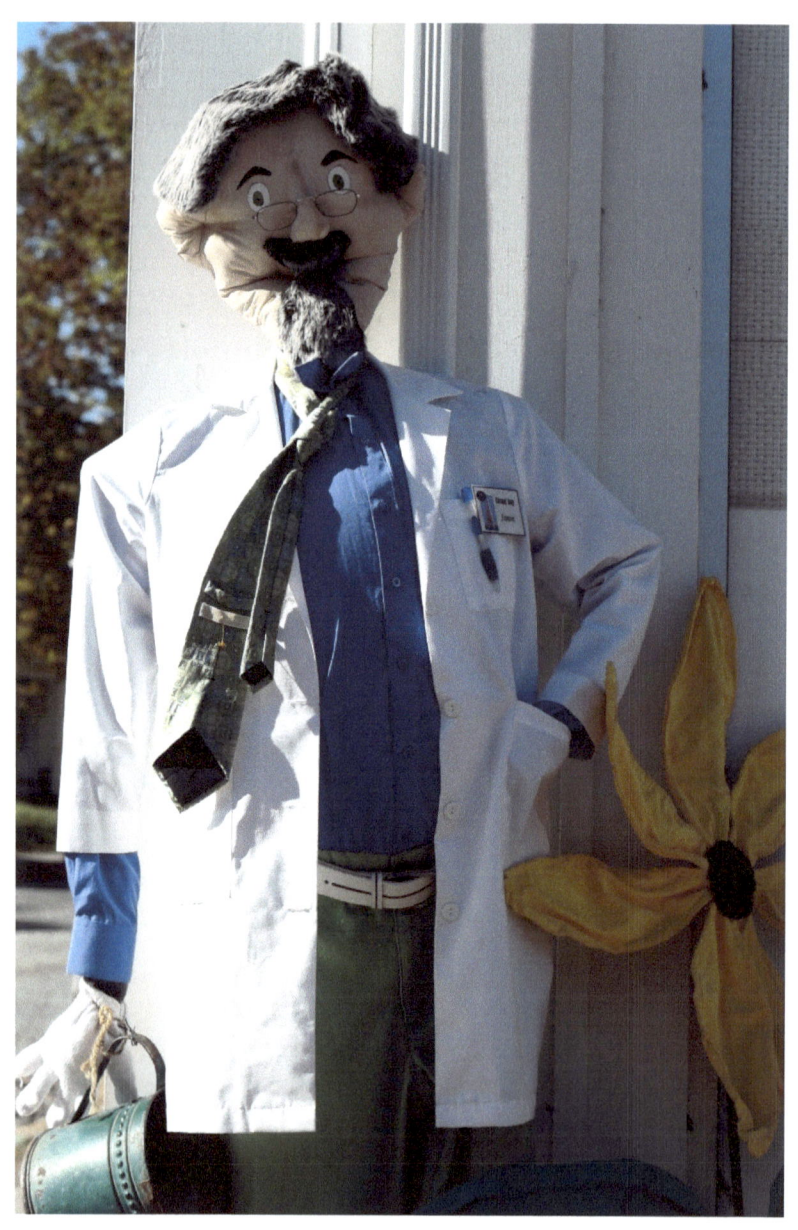

IN GERMANY, SCARECROWS LOOKED LIKE WOODEN WITCHES AND WERE ALLEGEDLY SUPPOSED TO HASTEN SPRING.

IN NEW YORK, A MAN CALLED ANDY MASLIN, PUT A SCARECROW OF 51 FEET TALL IN A PARK NAMED CHASE MILLS. IT WAS LIKELY THE TALLEST SCARECROW THAT HAS EVER BEEN MADE.

IN PARTS OF IRELAND, SCARECROWS REPRESENTED POLITICAL PERSUASIONS. ULSTER SCARECROWS THAT NATIONALISTS HAD WORE GREEN AND WERE TOPPED WITH BLACK BERETS. WHEREAS SCARECROWS OWNED BY ORANGEMEN FACED BELFAST.

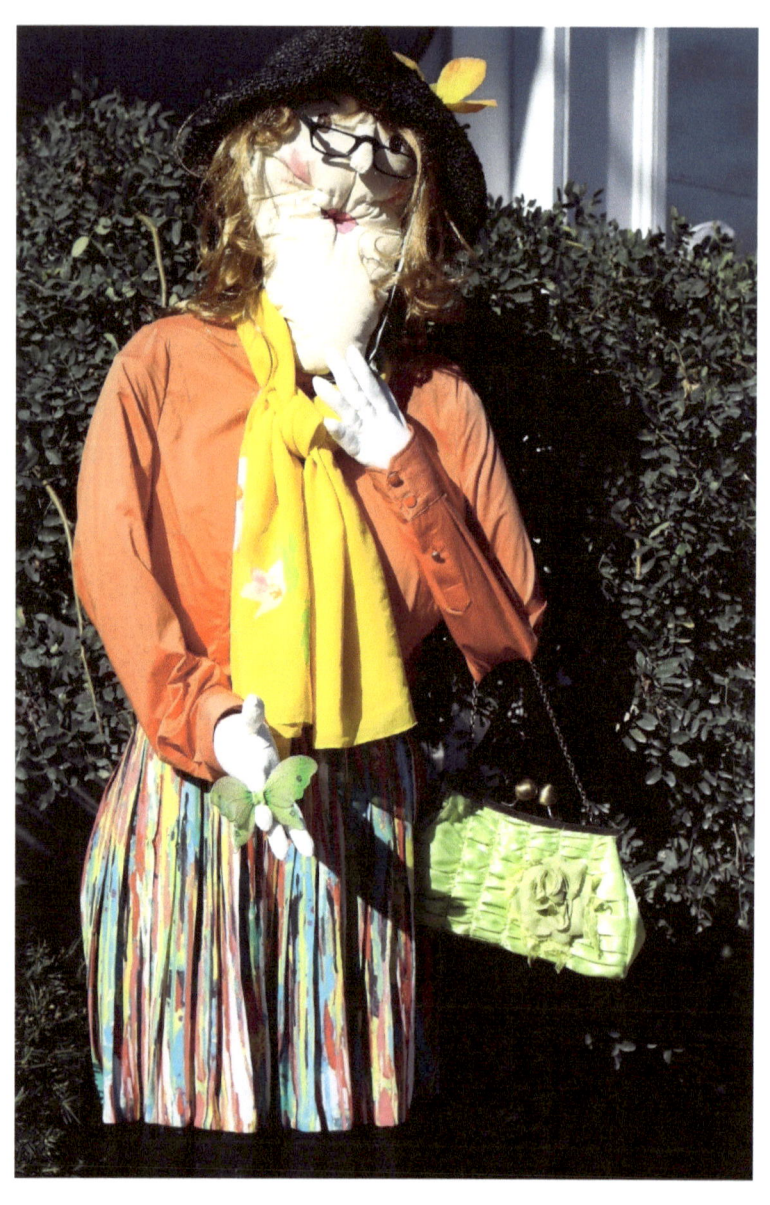

NATIVE AMERICANS HAD ADULT MEN GUARDING THEIR CORN FIELDS. CREEK NATIVES IN GEORGIA USED STRAW HUTS TO STAY IN SO THAT THEY COULD PROTECT THEIR GROWING CROPS.

"SOME REGIONAL NAMES OF SCARECROWS IN INDIA - KAG-DARAWA (HINDI), KAKTARUA (BENGALI), NOKK UKUTHI (MALAYALAM), SOLA KOLLA BOMMAI (TAMIL), DRISHTI BOMMAI (TELUGU), BUJGAAVANE (MARATHI), CHADIYO (GUJRATI), BUNGKYAACHAA (NEPALI)."

(http://bongroute.in/index.php/2016/03/22/scarecrow-10-interesting-facts/)

SCARECROWS THAT WERE IN DONEGAL, IRELAND HAD SHIRTS, OVERCOATS, AND EVEN NECK TIES. THEY WERE CALLED "DANDIES."

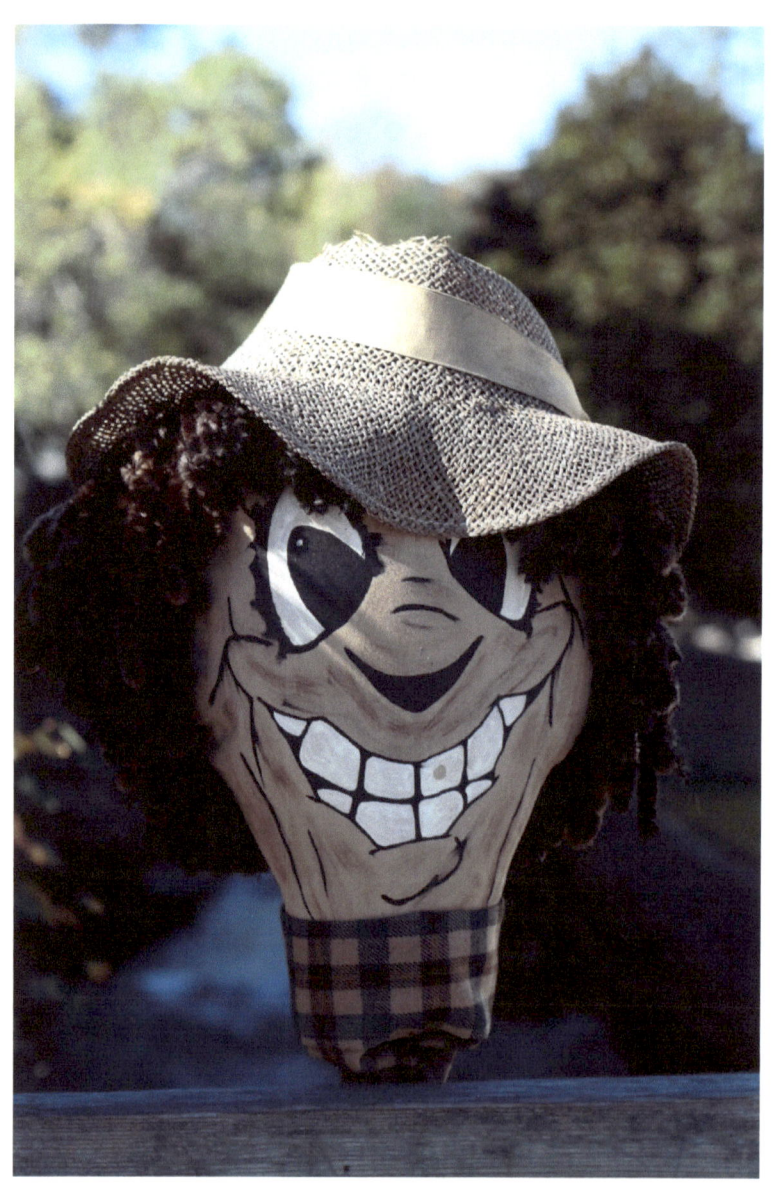

DURING THE "DIRTY THIRTIES" IT WAS COMMON TO SEE SCARECROWS IN EVERY GARDEN. HOWEVER, AFTER THE SECOND WORLD WAR CROPS WERE SPRAYED WITH DDT. SOME FARMERS TODAY USE WINDMILLS OR MECHANICAL, WHIRLING OBJECTS TO KEEP THAT BIRDS AWAY. IT IS RARE TO SEE A SCARECROW IN A BACKYARD GARDEN TODAY.

CROWS CONGREGATE IN GROUPS OF 20-30 AT THE SAME PLACE EACH NIGHT. THEREFORE, IT IS EXPEDIENT TO HAVE A SCARECROW ON GUARD AROUND THE CLOCK, SO THE CROPS WON'T BE EATEN.

THE CHILDREN THAT SURVIVED THE PLAGUE WERE USED AS LIVE SCARECROWS AND RAN AROUND UP TO THREE ACRES OF FARM TO SCARE BIRDS AWAY. THEY USED 2-3 WOODEN PIECES TIED TOGETHER THAT WERE CALLED "CLAPPERS". THIS MADE A NOISE THAT MADE PESKY BIRDS FLY AWAY.

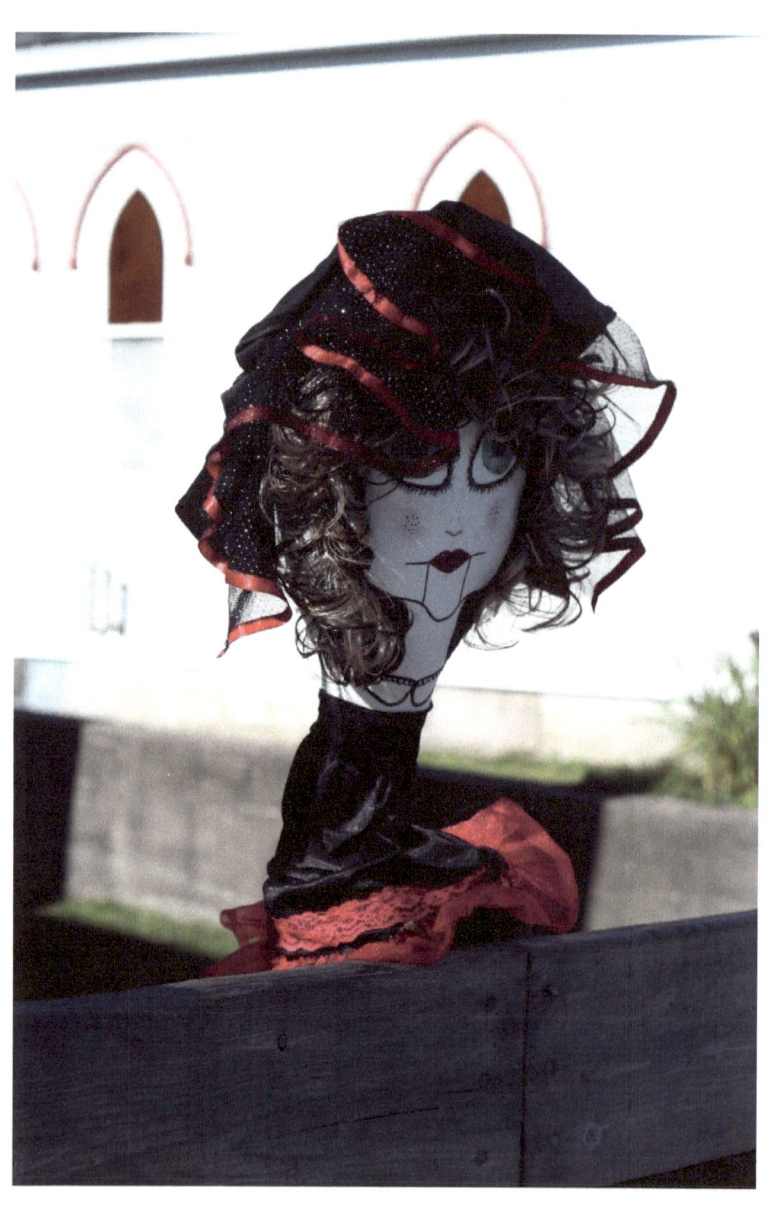

IN "SCARECROWS, HISTORICALLY SPEAKING, KATHY WARNES WRITES, "SCARECROWS HAVE EVOLVED ALONG WITH PEOPLE AND PEOPLE SPONSOR SCARECROW FESTIVALS EVERY YEAR IN PLACES AS DIVERSE AS WEST KILBRIDE, SCOTLAND, ST. CHARLES, ILLINOIS, AND ALBERTA, CANADA., MAHONE BAY, NOVA SCOTIA, ETC."

(http://historybecauseitshere.weebly.com/scarecrows-historically-speaking.html)

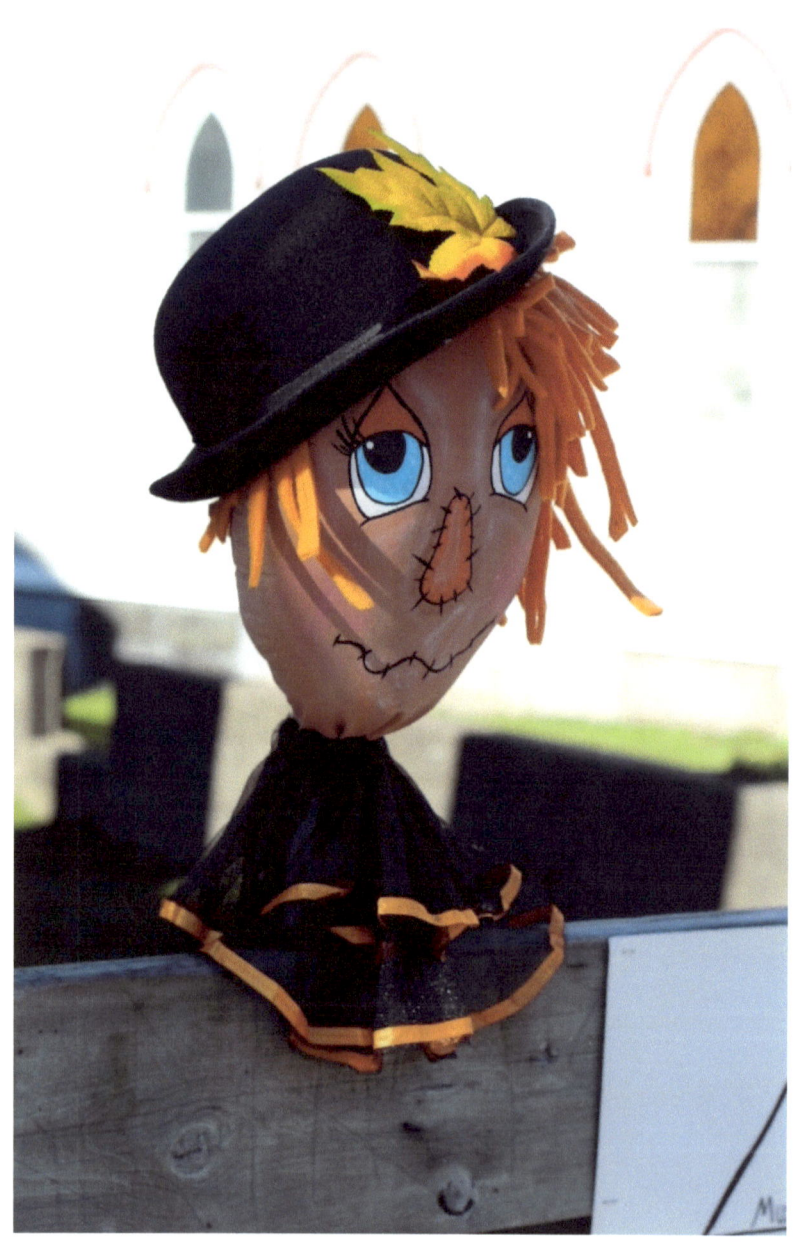

SOME HORROR MOVIES ABOUT SCARECROWS ARE "DARK NIGHT OF THE SCARECROW" (1981 TV MOVIE); "NIGHT OF THE SCARECROW" (1995); "MESSENGERS 2: THE SCARECROW" (2009 VIDEO); "HALLOWED GROUND" (2007 VIDEO); "SCARECROW" (2002 VIDEO); "SCARECROW SLAYER" (2003 VIDEO); "SCARECROW GONE WILD" (2004 VIDEO); AND "CHILDREN OF THE CORN III: URBAN HARVEST" (1995). A LOT OF HORROR MOVIES SHOW THAT EVIL DEEDS ARE DONE IN A CORNFIELD.

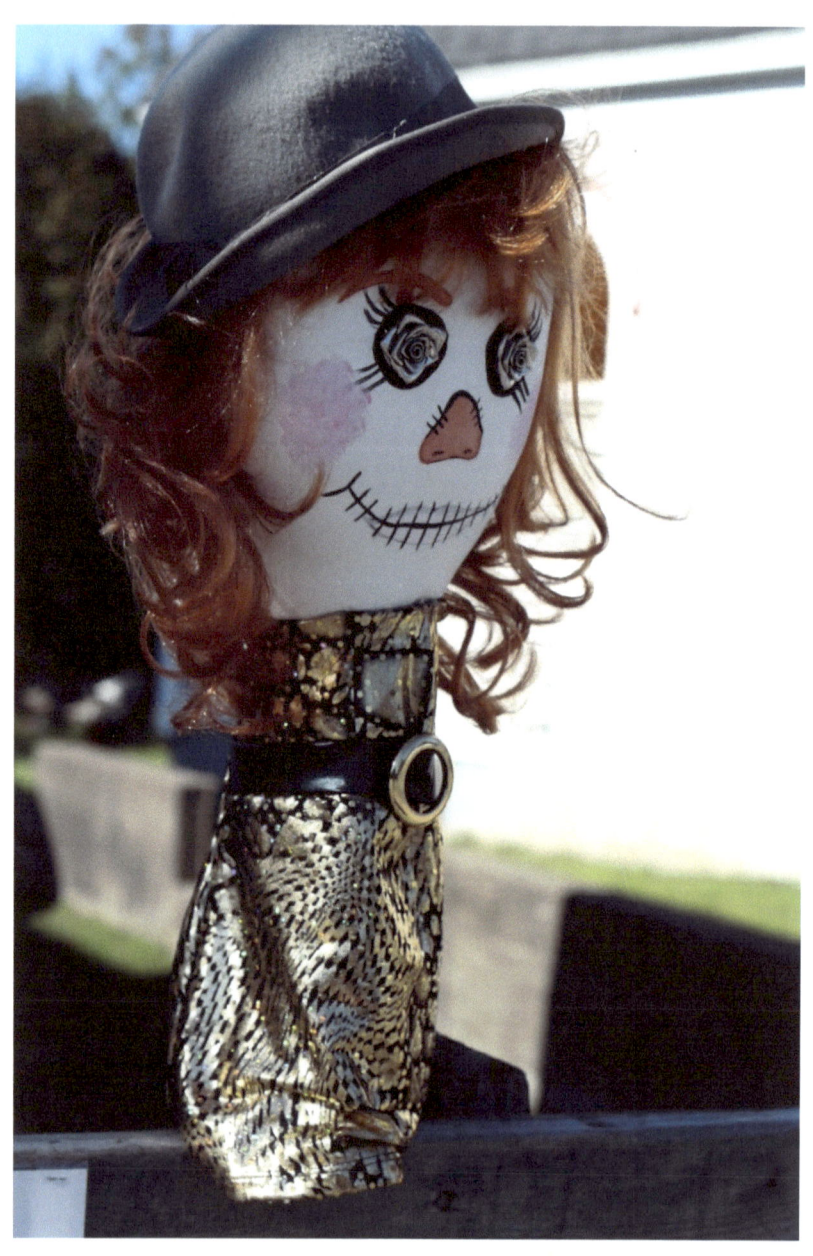

HOW DO YOU BUILD A SCARECROW? THE SKY IS THE LIMIT, BUT IF YOU WANT ONE THAT LOOKS LIKE A HUMAN DO THE FOLLOWING;

1. GET 2 STAKES AND NAIL THEM INTO A CROSS. POUND THIS INTO THE GROUND.

2. GET SOME WOMEN'S OR MEN'S CLOTHING AND DRESS THE SCARECROW.

3. STUFF THE CLOTHING WITH HAY OR STRAW.

4. PUT WORK BOOTS OR SHOES ON YOUR CREATION AND SEW OR PIN THEM ON.

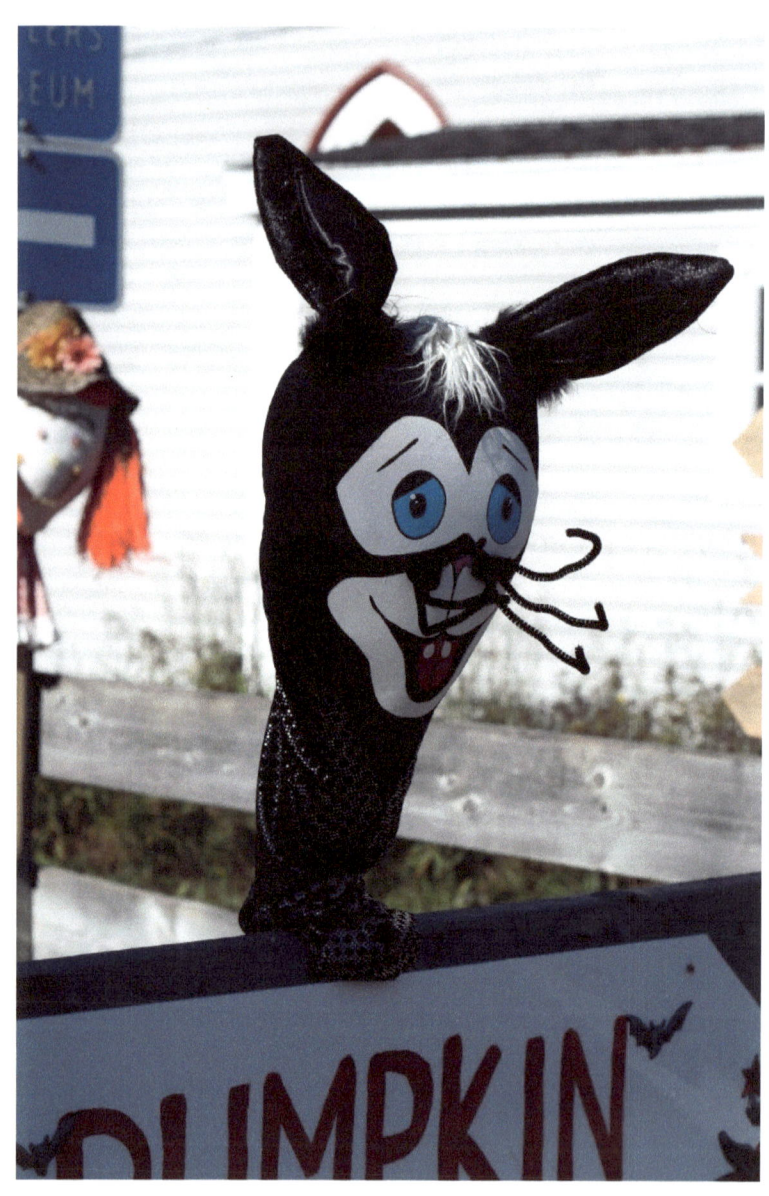

"THE LITTLE SCARECROW BOY" BY MARGARET WISE BROWN IS A CHILDREN'S STORY ABOUT A YOUNG SCARECROW WHOSE FATHER CLAIMS IS NOT FEROCIOUS ENOUGH TO SCARE A CROW.

THE JAPANESE VILLAGE OF NAGORO HAS 35 CITIZENS IN IT, HOWEVER, THERE ARE 150 SCARECROWS DWELLING THERE. TSUKIJI AYANO MADE THE LIFELIKE SCARECROWS. SHE CREATED 350 DOLLS. IT STARTED WHEN HER FATHER DIED, AND THE BIRDS ATE HER GARDEN. SHE MADE SCARECROWS TO PROTECT HER CROPS AND HOPED THAT HER FATHER'S SPIRIT WOULD HELP TOO.

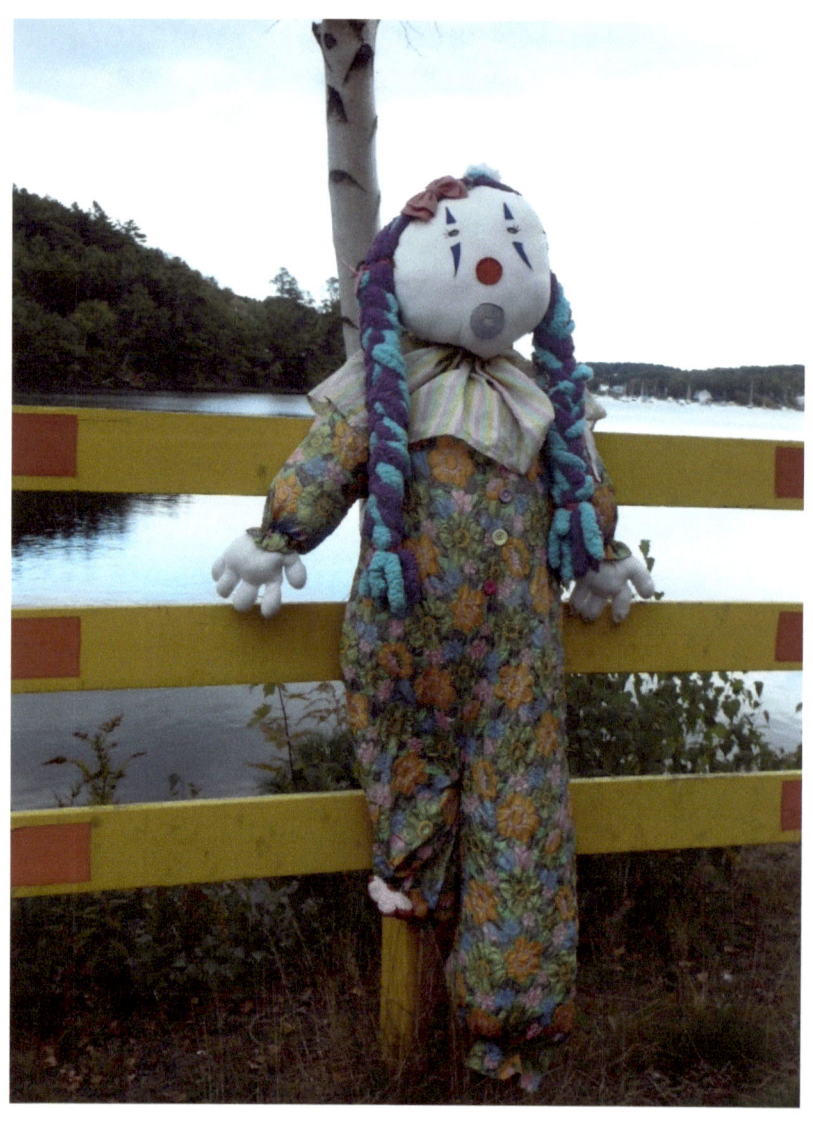

"THE SCAREBIRD" BY SID FLIESHMAN IS A CHILDREN'S STORY OF HOW A WEARY, FRIENDLESS FARMER BEFRIENDS HIS SCARECROW AND FINDS FRIENDSHIP AND LOVE.

IN THE QUIET FISHING TOWN OF MAHONE BAY, NOVA SCOTIA THE SCARECROW FESTIVAL HAS BEEN GOING ON EVERY FALL FOR 21 YEARS. TWENTY VOLUNTEERS HAVE MADE OVER 200 LIFE-SIZED SCARECROWS. THE INVENTIVE SCARECROWS ARE MADE INTO THE SHAPE OF MOUNTIES, HAREM LADIES, A PHARMACIST, A SCOTTISH MAN WITH HIS SHEEP, ETC. THEY ARE VERY ARTISTIC AND WELL DONE.

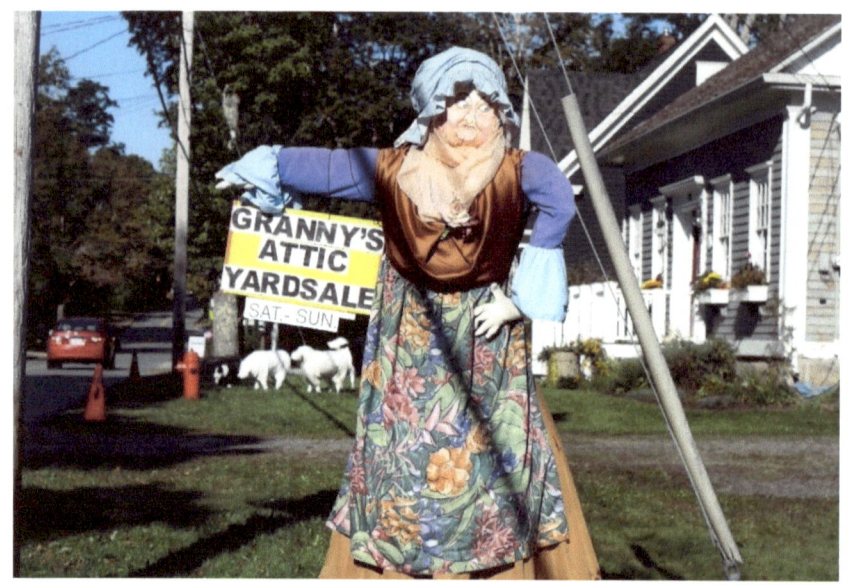

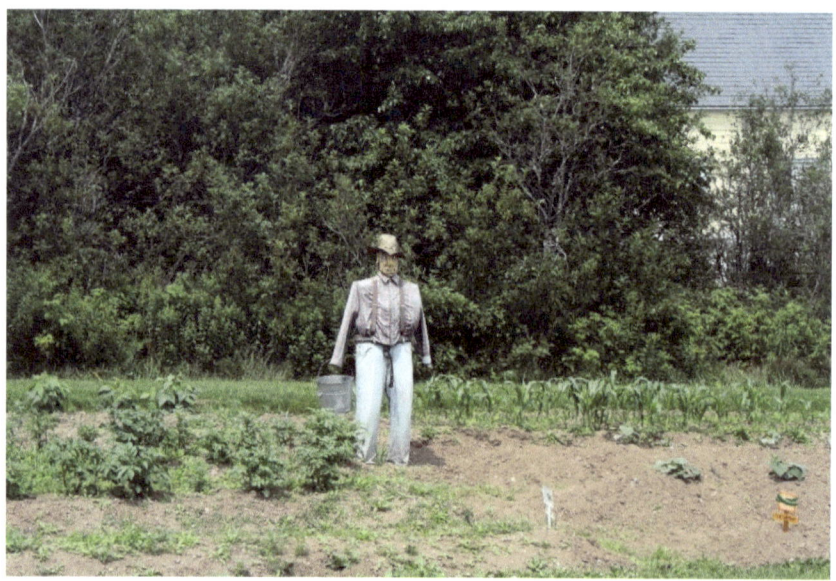

ALBANIA HAS A RICH CULTURAL HERITAGE AND HOLDS A STRANGE BELIEF ABOUT SCARECROWS. THEY APPEAR IN STRANGE PLACES AND ARE EITHER HUNG OR IMPALED WITH A ROD. THE ALBANIANS THINK THAT IF A BUILDING IS BEING BUILT, A SCARECROW WILL KEEP THE NEIGHBORS FROM HARMING IT. TEDDY BEARS ARE ALSO HUNG OR IMPALED FOR THE SAME REASON. IN SHORT, SCARECROWS ARE SUPPOSED TO BRING GOOD LUCK.

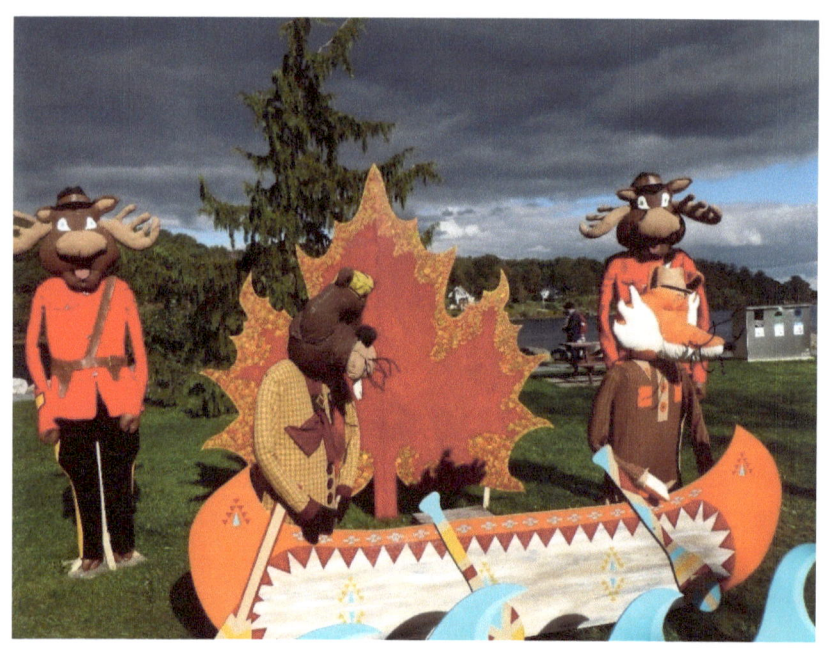

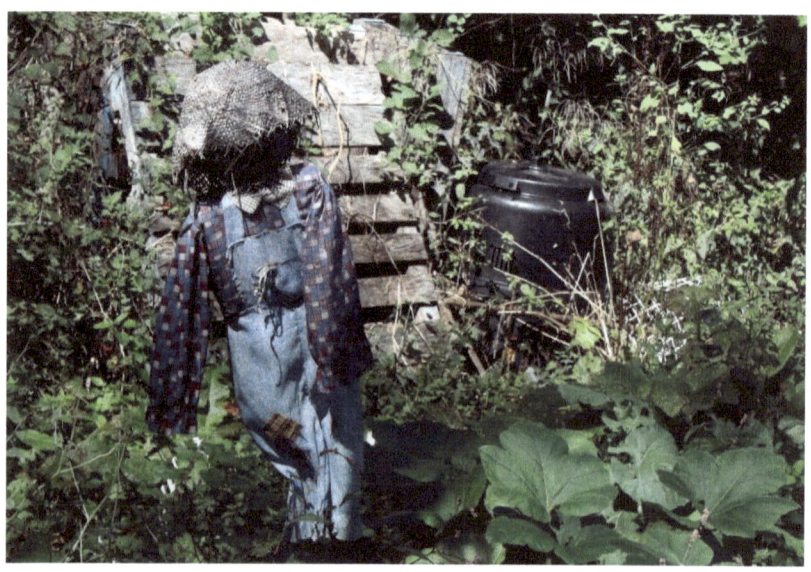

HERE IS A RECIPE FOR "SCARECROW SCRAMBLE" FOUND AT:

(http://www.cdkitchen.com/recipes/recs/1751/Scarecrow-Scramble84118.shtm)

THE SCARIEST SCARECROWS IN THE WORLD OCCURRED DURING WORLD WAR II WHEN FINLAND WAS FIGHTING RUSSIA. THE FINNS USED PSYCHOLOGICAL WARFARE, BY PROPPING UP THE FALLEN RUSSIAN SOLDIERS, SO THAT THEIR COMRADES WOULD SEE THEIR FROZEN FRIENDS FACING THEM.

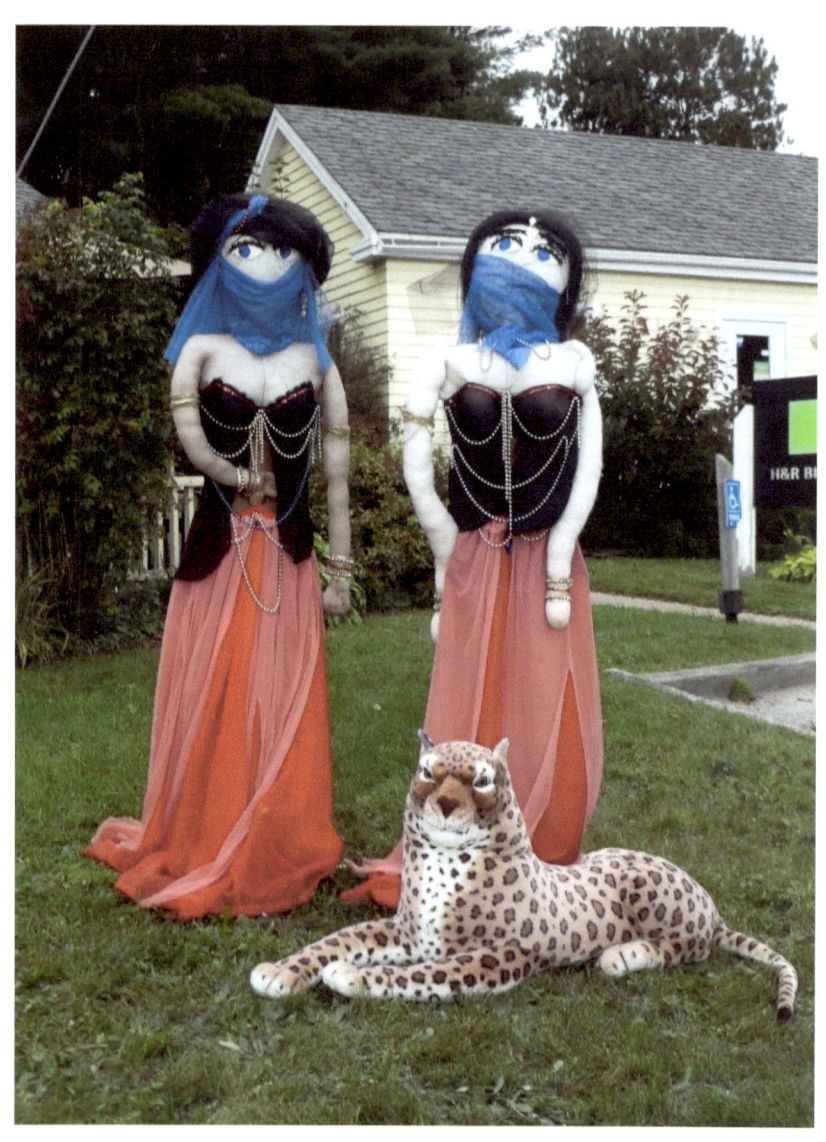

SCARECROWS ARE ALSO CALLED JACKS-OF-STRAW; SCAREBIRDS; TATTY BOGLES; AND SHOY-HOYS?

HUNGARY IS USING SCARY MASKS CARVED OUT OF SUGAR BEET ROOT AS SCARECROWS THAT ARE PLACED BY THEIR BORDERS. THIS IS TO STEM THE TIDE OF SYRIAN REFUGEES. THE AVERAGE HUNGARIAN IS NOT ALLOWED NEAR THE BORDER, BUT THE MASKS HAVE BEEN REPORTED BY A HUNGARIAN JOURNALIST AND UPLOADED ON FACEBOOK.

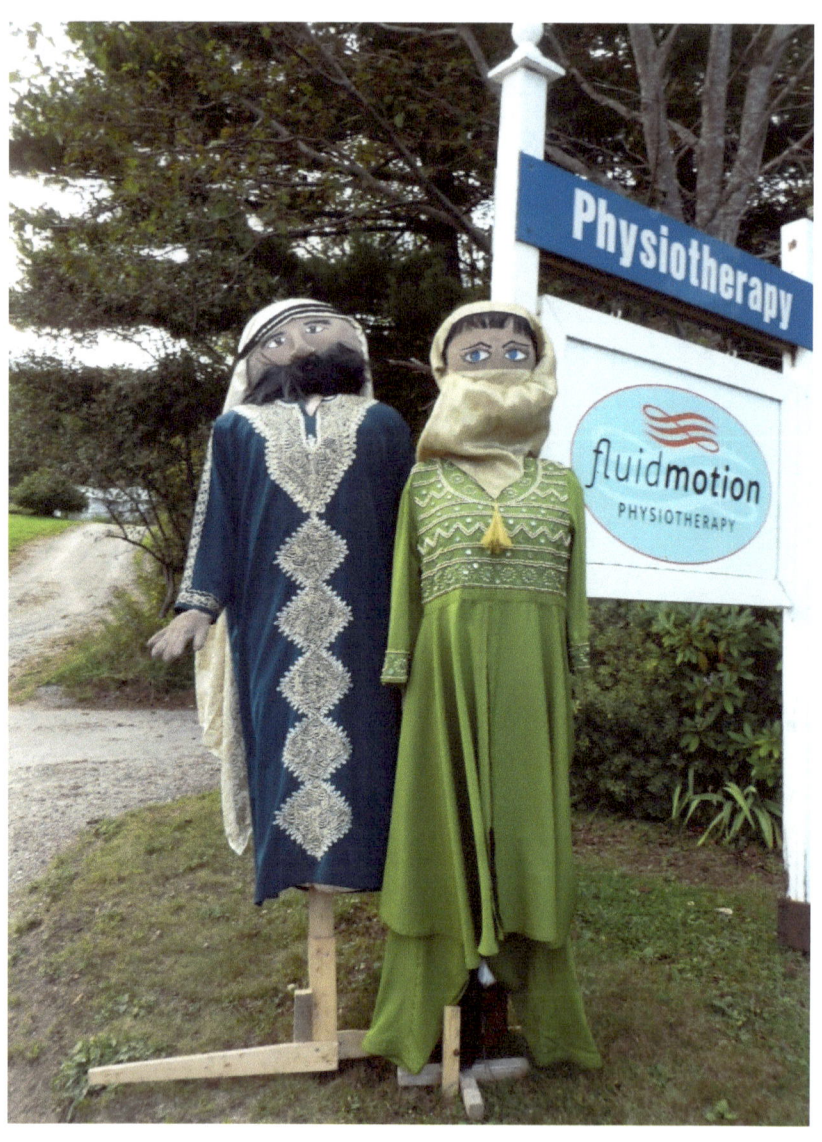

EATON VILLAGE IN ENGLAND HAS SOME
INTERESTING NAMES FOR THEIR
SCARECROWS:

QUEEN OF HEARTS;

QUEEN BEE;

KING NEPTUNE;

HENRY VIII;

QUEEN JUBY;

KING OF THE FOOD;

ROYAL MINT;

AND TATTLE ARE A FEW.

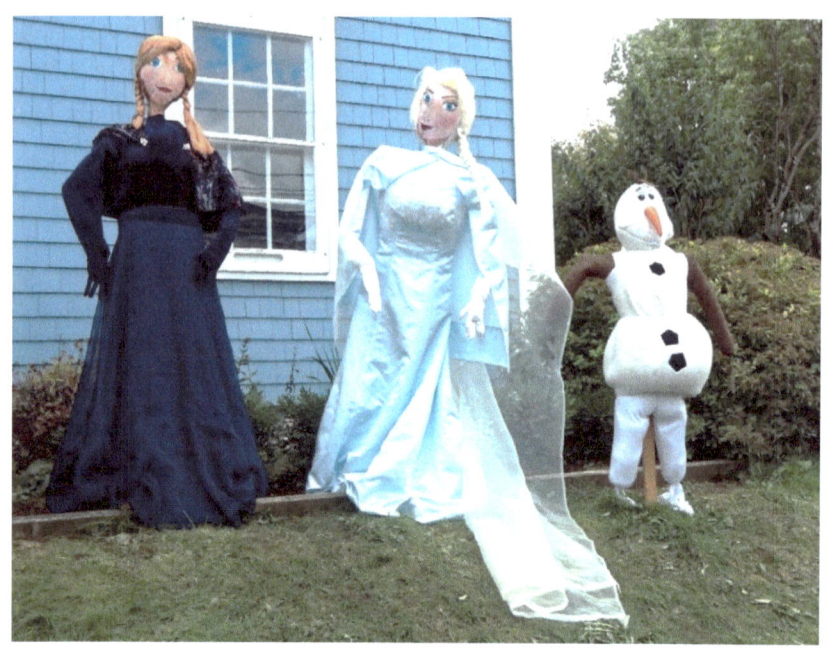

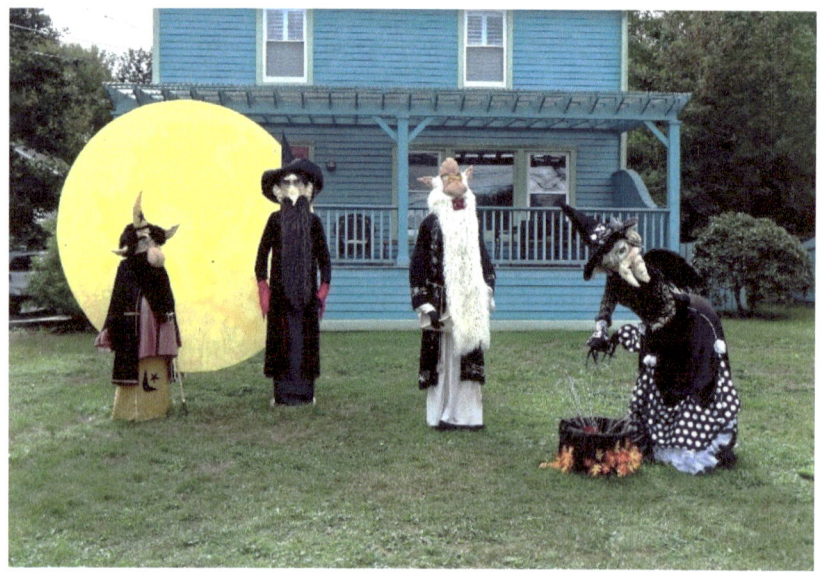

TO IMPROVE THE CHANCES OF DETERRING PEST BIRDS LIKE CROWS, MOVING THE SCARECROW AROUND HELPS. SCARECROWS THAT HAVE REALISTIC FACIAL FEATURES AND BRIGHT CLOTHING ARE MORE EFFECTIVE THAN THOSE THAT DON'T HAVE THAT. THE BEST PROTECTION, HOWEVER, COMES FROM SCARECROWS THAT MOVE.

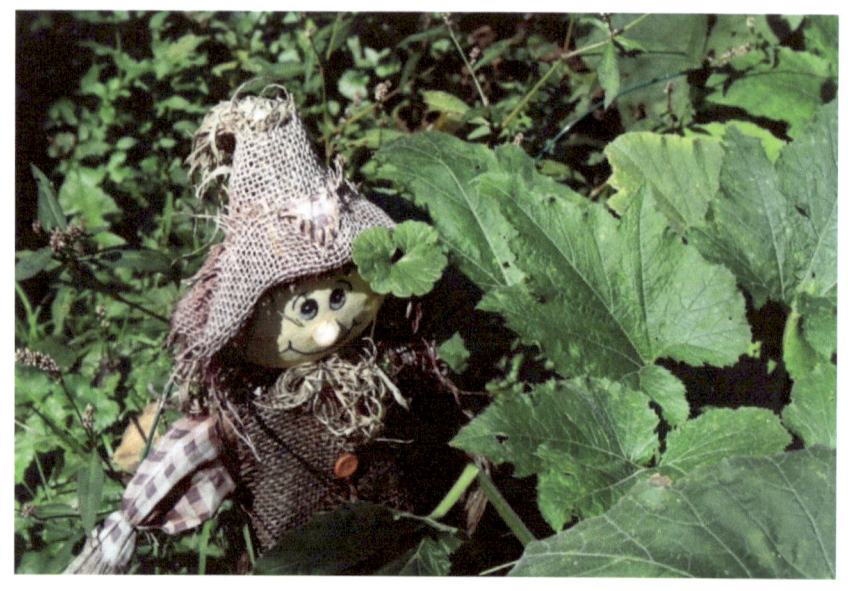
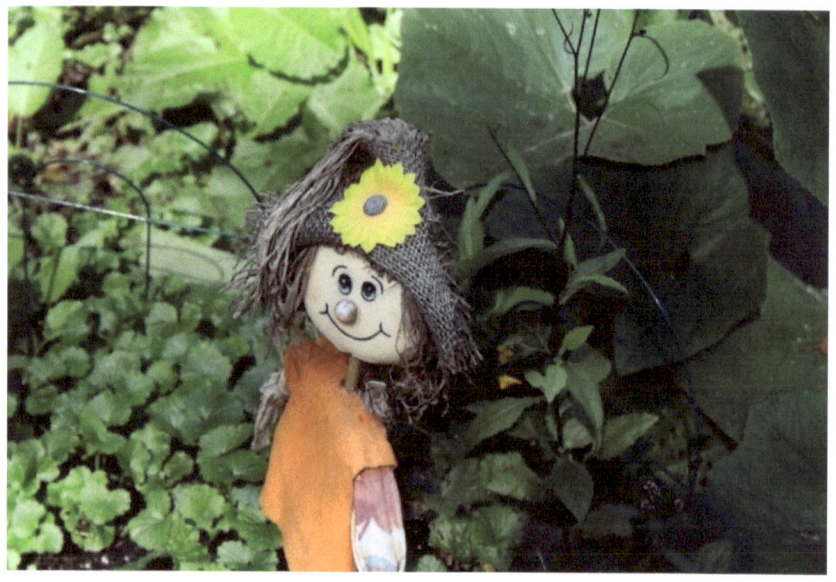

TODAY'S TECHNOLOGY HAS DEVELOPED THE "DIGITAL SCARECROW" THAT CAN SENSE WHEN AN ANIMAL OR BIRD IS APPROACHING AND EMITS A HARMLESS SUPERSONIC WAVE. IT CAN SURVEY 178,000 SQUARE FEET OF FARMLAND.

ANOTHER HIGH-TECH SCARECROW THAT FARMERS NOW USE IS SOMETHING CALLED AN "AGRILASER" THAT EMITS LASER BEAMS. IT IS NOISELESS, AND THE BIRDS DON'T SEEM TO GET USED TO THE LASER.

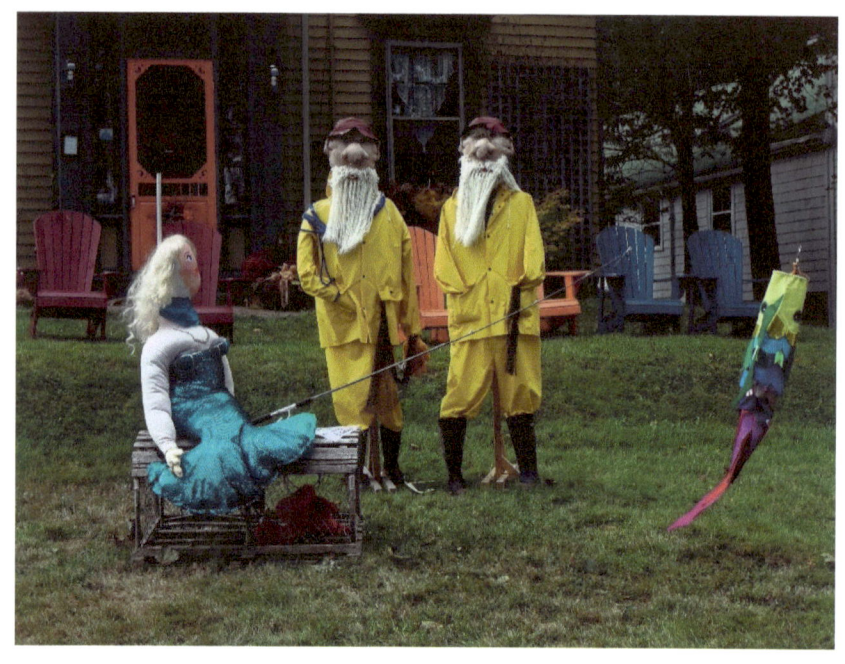

DO SCARECROWS ACTUALLY WORK? WHILE SOME BIRDS GET USED TO STATIONARY SCARECROWS, THERE WAS A STUDY DONE IN 1980 THAT SHOWED 95% OF DUCKS DISAPPEARED FROM A POND WHEN EXPOSED TO A SCARECROW.

"THE SCARECROW'S HAT" BY KEN BROWN IS A CHILDREN'S STORY ABOUT A CHICKEN WHO WANTS TO MAKE A NEST OUT OF THE SCARECROWS HAT, BUT MUST SHARE WITH A BUNCH OF OTHER ANIMALS SUCH AS BADGER, CROW, SHEEP, OWL. AND DONKEY.

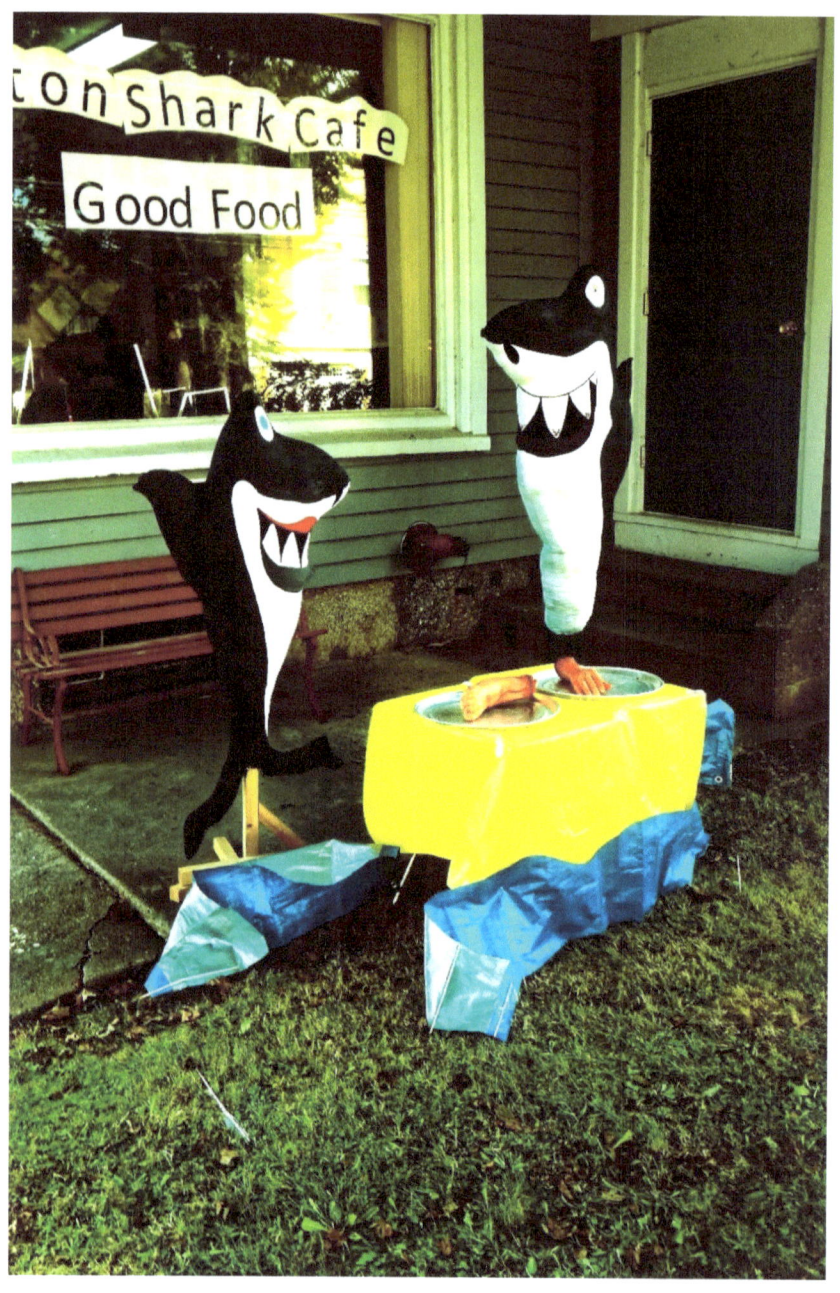

ALTHOUGH THE TRADITIONAL SCARECROW HAS A LOT OF NOSTALGIA ATTACHED TO IT, BIRDS EVENTUALLY BECOME DESENSITIZED AND CONTINUE EATING CROPS. HOWEVER, A DUTCH COMPANY, CALLED "CLEAR FLIGHT SOLUTIONS" HAS INVENTED "ROBIRDS" WHICH ARE 3-D FALCONS. THESE ROBIRDS FRIGHTEN SMALLER BIRDS IN AIRPORTS AND ON FARMS.

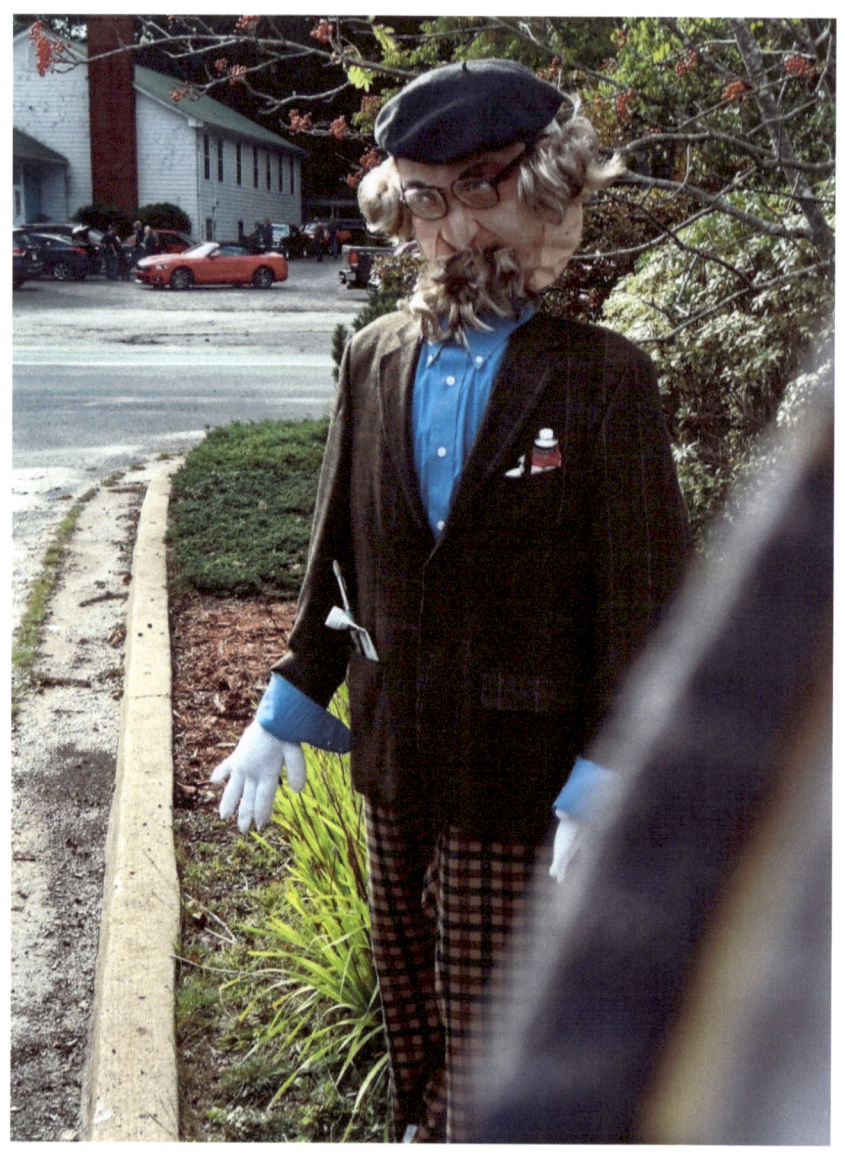

CHILDREN WERE USED AS LIVE SCARECROWS (BIRD CHASERS) ON FARMS UP UNTIL THE 1800'S, WHEN MINING AND FACTORY WORK PAID THEM MORE MONEY.

AFTER THE BLACK DEATH, THAT KILLED HALF THE POPULATION OF BRITAIN, FARMERS COULDN'T FIND ENOUGH PEOPLE TO SCARE THE BIRDS AWAY. THEREFORE, THEY TOOK SACKS AND FILLED THEM FULL OF STRAW. THEN THEY CARVED A FACE OUT OF A GOURD OR TURNIP. THE RESULT WAS THE FIRST BRITISH SCARECROW.

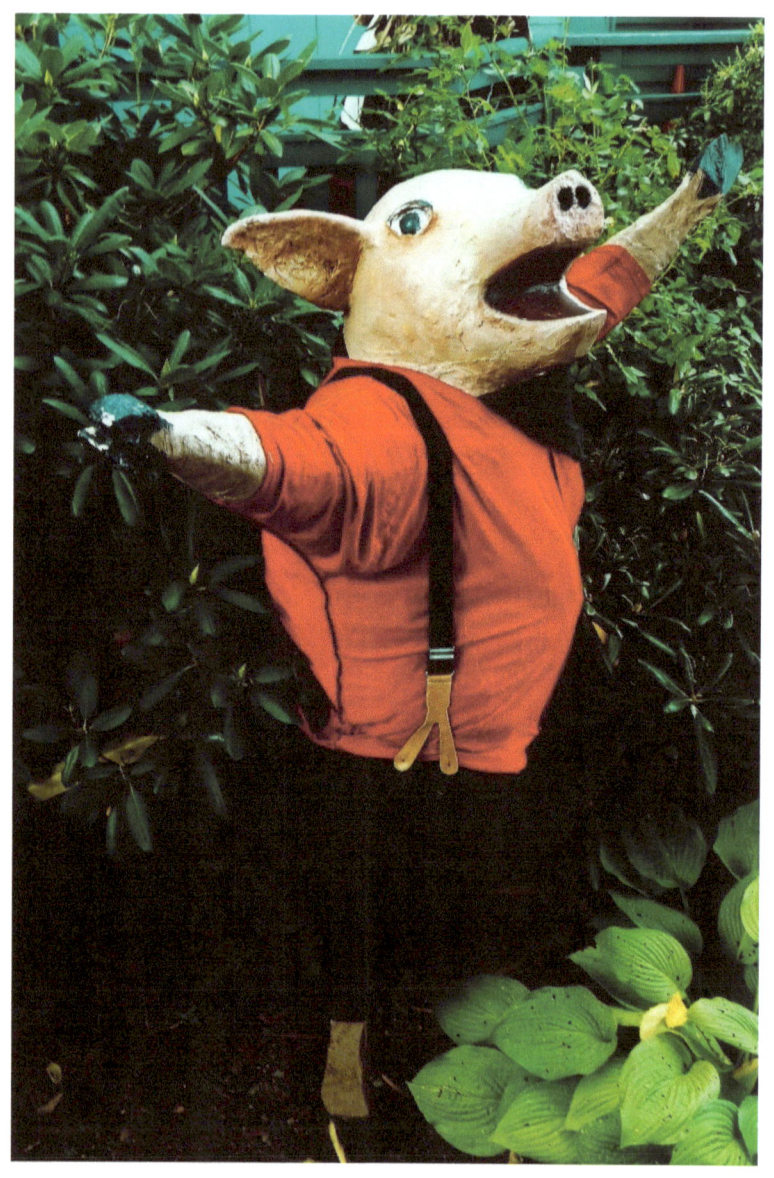

www.ingramcontent.com/pod-product-compliance
Lightning Source LLC
Chambersburg PA
CBHW040238220526
45473CB00001B/282